The Daily Examen Journal

A 30-Day Spiritual Retreat

Jerry Windley-Daoust

The Daily Examen Journal:
A 30-Day Spiritual Retreat

Copyright ©2020 by Jerry Windley-Daoust. All rights reserved.
No part of this book may be reproduced by any means without
the written permission of the publisher.

Printed in the United States of America.

Copy editing by Karen Carter.
Book design by Jerry Windley-Daoust.

All images licensed from Adobe Stock.

Scripture quotations are from New Revised Standard Version Bible: Catholic Edition,
copyright © 1989, 1993 National Council of the Churches of Christ in the United States of America.
Used by permission. All rights reserved worldwide.

First Edition: 2020

ISBN 978-1-944008-57-4

If you would like to continue using *The Daily Examen Journal*
beyond the thirty entries in this book, you can download
a color PDF edition from gracewatch.org/journals.

GRACEWATCH MEDIA
Winona, Minnesota
gracewatch.org

Prayers to Accompany the Examen

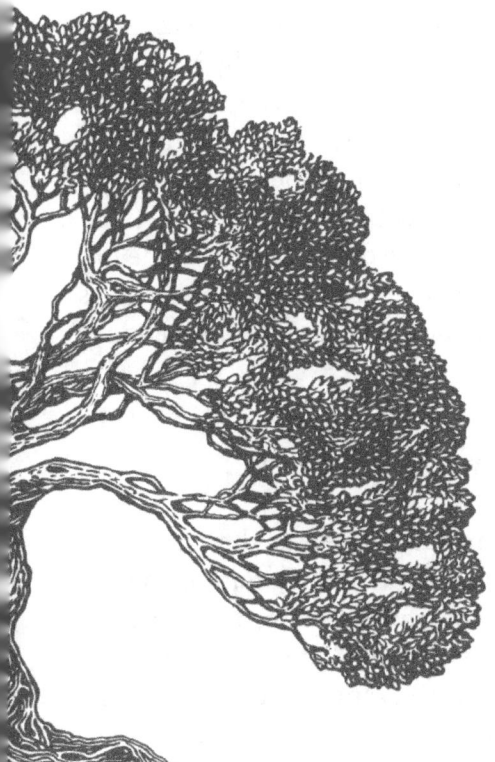

ANIMA CHRISTI

Soul of Christ, sanctify me.
Body of Christ, save me.
Blood of Christ, inebriate me.
Water from the side of Christ, wash me.
Passion of Christ, strengthen me.
O good Jesus, hear me.
Within thy wounds hide me.
Suffer me not to be separated from thee.
From the malignant enemy defend me.
In the hour of my death call me.
And bid me come unto thee,
that with thy Saints I may praise thee
forever and ever.

Amen.

SUSCIPE

Receive, O Lord, all my liberty.
Take my memory, understanding, and entire will.
Whatever I have or possess you have given me;
I restore it all to you, and surrender it wholly to be
governed by your will. Give me love for you alone
along with your grace, and I am rich enough,
and ask for nothing more.

Amen.

Introduction

The Importance of Paying Attention

When writer Annie Dillard was a child growing up in Pittsburgh, she used to hide pennies along the sidewalk for someone else to find, sometimes tucked in between the roots of an old tree. Once a penny was hidden, she would chalk arrows on the sidewalk directing passersby to the treasure. Sometimes she would even write encouraging little notes, such as SURPRISE AHEAD or MONEY THIS WAY. The thought of some lucky stranger discovering this treasure delighted her.

Sadly, she gave up the practice as she grew up, but she told the story in her award-winning book, *A Pilgrim at Tinker Creek*, to make a point: "The world is fairly studded and strewn with pennies cast broadside from a generous hand." All we need is to keep our eyes wide open for the copper glint of the pennies, she says. If we practice patient watchfulness, we will find our days full of riches.

St. Ignatius of Loyola (1491–1556), the Spanish soldier turned spiritual warrior, may have appreciated Dillard's spirit. In his case, though, it was not pennies he was after, but the pearl without price, the treasure in the field—the very presence of God, casting grace into his life from a generous hand. He took seriously Jesus' admonition to "keep awake" for the coming of the Lord (Matthew 24:42). And by this standard, by the end of his life, he could account himself a rich man; as he said in his *Autobiography*, "Whenever he wished, at whatever hour, he could find God."

This spiritual richness, this sensitivity to God's presence, didn't just happen. Instead, it was the fruit of his daily practice of prayerfully reflecting on God's movement within the deepest part of his heart. Fortunately for the rest of us, St. Ignatius taught this practice to the members of the religious order he founded, the Society of Jesus ("the Jesuits"). The practice he developed has come to be known as the Ignatian Examen (also known as the Daily Examen, or the Examen/examination of consciousness).

What Is the Examen?

As its Latin name suggests, the examen prayer is a spiritual self-examination, the purpose of which is to become more conscious of the movement of God in the everyday events of our lives. We examine our own feelings, thoughts, words, and actions in each part of the day, asking: "Where was God in this moment? Where was I?" Over time, this practice of "waking up" to God also awakens us to our true self ... the fullness of the person God calls us to be.

The Ignatian Examen is different from the examination of conscience that Catholics are taught to do in preparation for celebrating the sacrament of Penance and Reconciliation. Typically, an examination of conscience involves reviewing one's actions in order to bring to light any sins or shortcomings. These can then be brought to confession for forgiveness and healing.

While the Ignatian Examen might also reveal things for which we need to seek God's healing, its scope is much broader. In the Examen, Jesus

"The world is fairly studded & strewn with pennies cast broadside by a generous hand."

invites us to cast our nets into "deep water" (Luke 5:4), exploring our relationship with God in all its dimensions. We not only ask, "How did I live today?" but also, "What moved me to live the way I did? Was I moved by God or by something else?"

The ultimate purpose of this prayerful, Spirit-guided examination is to become more and more sensitive to God's presence and promptings within us, not only while we are praying the Examen, but all the time. And as we get better at recognizing God's presence throughout our days, it becomes easier to more lovingly respond to his many gifts in our thoughts, words, and actions.

When should you pray the Examen? Although Jesuits are required to pray the Examen twice a day, once at midday and once in the evening, most lay people pray it once a day. You can pray it at any time of day that is convenient; if you pray it at some time other than in the evening, simply review the period since you last did an examen (or the previous twenty-four hours). Most people allow about fifteen minutes to do the Examen well; in a pinch, it can be abbreviated.

Here is an overview of the six movements of the Examen as they are proposed in this journal:

1. **Pray for enlightenment.** Begin your time of prayer by asking the Holy Spirit to accompany you during the Examen and to bring to your attention whatever will help your spiritual growth.
2. **Give thanks.** Review your day in a spirit of gratitude for the many gifts God has given to you.
3. **Examine your thoughts, words, and actions.** Next, review your day more systematically, hour by hour, focusing on your thoughts, words, and actions in relation to yourself, others, and God.
4. **Respond to God in prayer.** Offer to God those key moments with a prayer of gratitude or contrition.
5. **Make resolutions for tomorrow.** Using insights from the previous movements as a springboard, resolve to live more fully in Christ tomorrow.
6. **Conclude in prayer.** Finish with the Our Father or another short prayer.

Below, we'll look at the spirit and intent of each of these movements in greater detail. But, before we do that, let's briefly talk about writing your prayer in this journal.

Journaling the Examen

The *Daily Examen Journal* invites you to journal your Examen prayer experience in daily entries. St. Ignatius kept a cherished notebook of his spiritual insights, and he encouraged his Jesuits to keep simple written notes recording their spiritual progress. This is one of the advantages of journaling your prayer: it provides a record of your spiritual journey that you can reference later.

There are other benefits to writing down your prayer. If you are easily distracted, writing can help you focus by slowing you down and taking your prayer deeper as you consider how to give concrete expression to your thoughts and feelings. A prayer journal is also a helpful accountability tool as you begin to establish a new prayer habit.

Having said all that, writing can also be an obstacle to prayer—a distraction in itself—especially if we're overly concerned with the technical quality of our writing. Don't worry about spelling, grammar, or the flow of the words on the page. If writing isn't usually your thing, you might think of it as simply taking notes, jotting down a few words that capture your prayer experience.

Some people write as they pray, but, if this feels difficult, pray first, and then record your experience afterward. You may be surprised at the insights you glean from reflecting on your prayer time in this way.

The Six Movements of the Examen

Now let's take a closer look at the six movements of the Examen prayer. As with any commentary on prayer, the description that follows shouldn't be understood as a strict, one-size-fits-all recipe. Prayer is a conversation between God and an individual person, which means it is always unique. In fact, if you make the regular practice of the Examen a habit, its various movements will eventually flow more naturally under the prompting of the Holy Spirit.

1. Pray for Enlightenment

We begin the Examen by praying for the guiding light of the Holy Spirit. As Christians, we believe that the Holy Spirit "inspired" (or breathed life into) the sacred Tradition and Scriptures of the Church. But we also believe that this life-giving work of the Spirit continues in the Church—in each of us—today.

The first movement of the Examen, therefore, is to invite the Holy Spirit to enlighten your heart—to teach you, to breathe life into you—during this time of prayer.

Could you benefit from reflecting on your day on your own, without the help of the Holy Spirit? Surely many people do. But without the help of the Holy Spirit, our own pride, ignorance, or laziness may prevent us from seeing the truth about ourselves. If we are open to the help of the Holy Spirit, he will gradually, gently reveal our true selves to us. We should welcome this healing, nurturing light of the Holy Spirit because God desires nothing for us other than our ultimate happiness.

How do you invite the Holy Spirit to accompany you during this time of prayer? You might simply pray: "Holy Spirit, open my heart; enlighten me with your love, so that I might grow closer to you." You can, of course, use your own words to express this simple sentiment.

Besides praying these words, you might also spend a few moments settling down, quieting your mind to make room for the Spirit. Relax, restfully leaning into God's presence. Think of giving yourself over to God as a physical sensation similar to relaxing into a back float in the pool, or a kiss.

The first movement in this journal. You won't find any writing space provided for this step; instead, each entry includes a brief prayer from a saint or Scripture.

2. Give Thanks

Gratitude is the foundation of our relationship with God. In the second step, then, we thank God for the many gifts, both large and small, that we have received throughout the day.

Practicing gratitude puts us in right relationship with God. It acknowledges two fundamental truths:

1. We are nothing and have nothing in ourselves, nor are we "owed" anything.
2. God is everything, has blessed us with everything we have, and wishes to give us even more—all of himself.

Taking time every day to appreciate these truths helps us avoid the sins of ingratitude (taking God's gifts for granted) and resentment (sulking over not getting what we think we deserve).

The daily practice of gratitude gradually leads us to experience a deep spiritual joy in the realization that everything is a gift. And our natural response to this gift of "everything" is to praise and thank God.

St. Francis is famous for the extent to which he lived this spirit of gratitude and joy. Once when he and a companion were begging for alms, someone doused them with a bucket of cold, dirty water. His natural response was to give God thanks. And more remarkably, knowing St. Francis, his thanksgiving was probably genuine, not affected.

Where does that leave the rest of us? Some of us have bad days, bad weeks, or even a lifetime filled with more than our fair share of trouble and sorrow. Many of us also experience depression. We can hardly be expected to start out like St. Francis. But being attentive to God's gifts in our lives and giving him thanks is even more important in these circumstances. Going through the motions of naming God's gifts in our lives might be the best we can do, but it's a start, and we can do this while also praying for the Holy Spirit to help us feel real gratitude. We do so not for God's sake, but for our own sake—so that, even in the darkness, we might know the light of God's love.

The second movement in this journal. Under the label "Give thanks," write down the gifts you have received from God this day. How were you nourished today, both physically and spiritually?

3. Examine Your Thoughts, Words, and Actions

In the third movement, we examine our thoughts, words, and actions over the course of the day (or since the last time you did the Examen). Reviewing the day hour by hour, we remember how we acted toward God, others, and ourselves. We might ask:

- How have I treated myself today?
- How have I treated others in my thoughts, words, and actions?
- How have I connected (or not connected) with God today?

We're not so much counting up our moral victories and defeats as we are simply taking a clear-eyed look at our story as it unfolded today. We're practicing awareness, consciousness … keeping our eyes open, as Annie Dillard would say. This is the first step toward intentionality, the practice of consciously directing our actions. With consciousness comes freedom, and with freedom comes the ability to act according to God's love for us. This is the goal of the Examen.

Although what we say and do may be at the top of our mind during our review of the day, St. Ignatius is most concerned with our thoughts, attitudes, and feelings, because it is these that give rise to our words and actions. He takes his cue from Jesus: "The good person out of the good treasure of the heart produces good, and the evil person out of evil treasure produces evil; for it is out of the abundance of the heart that the mouth speak." (Luke 6:45)

As we review our day, then, we may at first focus on our words and actions. Prompted by the Holy Spirit, one or more of these may particularly grab our attention—perhaps a conflict we had with someone, our sour mood, or the way we responded to something bad happening to us. Or the Holy Spirit may direct our attention to a "high" moment—the joy we felt joking around with coworkers, some small kindness we did for a stranger, or a difficult moment handled with grace.

Our next move should be to ask: What was the driving force behind what I did or said? What thoughts or habits of the heart prompted me to act the way I did? With the help of the Holy Spirit, we are seeking to know the truth about ourselves so that we might grow into our true self, the fullness of the person God made us to be.

The third movement in this journal. What did you do today? How did you treat yourself, others, and God? Under the "Examine" label, journal one or more aspects of your day that stands out to you.

4. Respond in Prayer

After our clear-eyed, honest examination in the previous step, it is natural for us to respond in prayer to whatever the Holy Spirit has revealed to us.

Maybe our day has been full of spiritual "highs," moments when we've felt especially connected to God, and our actions have been truly free. If so, take a moment to celebrate and rejoice, praising and thanking God for his grace at work in your life.

On the other hand, our review of the day might reveal moments of sinfulness ... or, at the very least, moments when we have fallen short, failing to respond to God's call as fully as we should. These moments might cause us sorrow, but this sorrow ought to be tempered by gladness that the Holy Spirit is helping us to grow closer to God. We can respond in prayer by expressing our sorrow to God and asking his forgiveness.

A sense of guilt and sorrow is good as long as it leads us to seek God's help and healing. Shame or despair, on the other hand, drives us away from him and should be avoided. If you find that shame is causing problems in your spiritual life, seek the help of a pastor or spiritual director.

The fourth movement in this journal. What do you want to bring to God from your day? Under the "Respond" label, write a short prayer offering God gratitude for the highs of your day and asking for his forgiveness for the lows.

5. Resolve to Live More Fully in Christ Tomorrow

Next, we resolve to live more fully in Christ in the coming day. Our resolution(s) ought to be simple, specific, and grounded in the insights we gained from our review of the previous day. For example, if we fell short in the way we treated a spouse or coworker, we might resolve—in very specific terms—to do better the next day. Alternatively, we might imagine a creative way to build on our spiritual successes; if we're celebrating our heroic patience with the children today, we might resolve that tomorrow we will strive to go further by really appreciating them, perhaps even offering them a compliment.

The fifth movement in this journal. What resolution(s) do you wish to make for the coming day? Write them down under the "Resolve" label.

6. Conclude in Prayer

St. Ignatius reminds us that our resolutions to do better are always accomplished "with the help of God's grace." We can close our time of prayer by very deliberately asking the Holy Spirit to open our hearts to his grace in the coming day.

St. Ignatius suggests we conclude with the Our Father, but you could conclude with another favorite prayer, or just the sign of the cross.

In Closing

Prayer is the work of the Holy Spirit; it is dynamic, not static. The same is true of the Daily Examen. Over the centuries, various people have built on the foundation offered by St. Ignatius, proposing different ways to pray the Examen—emphasizing one aspect or another, or explaining its movements in new ways. If the Examen becomes a regular practice, you might benefit from reading about other approaches.

An excellent place to begin is IgnatianSpirituality.com, a website maintained by Loyola Press. The "Daily Examen" page at that website contains links to numerous helpful articles, videos, and apps. Two articles especially worth reading are "Consciousness Examen," a classic work by Fr. George Aschenbrenner, SJ (also available as a booklet called *Examination of Consciousness* from Loyola Press), and "A Method of Making the General Examen" from the Manresa Jesuit Spiritual Renewal Centre.

For a more in-depth description, see *The Examen Prayer: Ignatian Wisdom for Our Lives Today* by Fr. Timothy M. Gallagher, OMV (Crossroad, 2006, 192 pages).

In closing, let's pray the Suscipe, a beautiful prayer of abandonment proposed by St. Ignatius:

Receive, O Lord, all my liberty. Take my memory, understanding, and entire will. Whatever I have or possess you have given me; I restore it all to you, and surrender it wholly to be governed by your will. Give me love for you alone along with your grace, and I am rich enough, and ask for nothing more.

"Give me love for you alone along with your grace, and I am rich enough, and ask for nothing more."

DAY 1

PRAY

God, please reveal to us your sublime beauty

Dear God,
please reveal to us your sublime beauty
that is everywhere, everywhere, everywhere,
so that we will never again feel frightened.
My divine love, my love,
please let us touch your face.

St. Francis of Assisi

DATE

GIVE THANKS

What gifts have you received today? How have you been nourished, physically and spiritually?

EXAMINE

What did you do today? How did you treat yourself, others, and God?

DAY 1

God, please reveal to us your sublime beauty

RESPOND

What do you want to bring to God from your day?

RESOLVE

What resolution(s) do you wish to make for the coming day?

PRAY

Conclude by praying for God's grace in the coming day. You might do this by praying the Our Father, the Anima Christi, or the Suscipe prayer (see page 3).

DAY 2

PRAY

May our ears hear you, may our eyes behold you

Gracious and holy Father,
grant us the intellect to understand you,
reason to discern you, diligence to seek you,
wisdom to find you, a spirit to know you,
a heart to meditate upon you.
May our ears hear you, may our eyes behold you,
and may our tongues proclaim you.
Give us grace that our ways may be pleasing to you,
that we may have the patience to wait for you
and the perseverance to look for you.

St. Benedict

DATE

GIVE THANKS

What gifts have you received today? How have you been nourished, physically and spiritually?

EXAMINE

What did you do today? How did you treat yourself, others, and God?

DAY 2

May our ears hear you, may our eyes behold you

RESPOND

What do you want to bring to God from your day?

RESOLVE

What resolution(s) do you wish to make for the coming day?

PRAY

Conclude by praying for God's grace in the coming day. You might do this by praying the Our Father, the Anima Christi, or the Suscipe prayer (see page 3).

DAY 3

DATE

PRAY

O fire and deep well of charity!

O eternal Trinity
Eternal Trinity!
O fire and deep well of charity!
O you who are madly in love
with your creature!
O eternal truth!
O eternal fire!
O eternal wisdom!
Grant us
your gentle and eternal benediction.
Amen.

St. Catherine of Siena

GIVE THANKS

What gifts have you received today? How have you been nourished, physically and spiritually?

EXAMINE

What did you do today? How did you treat yourself, others, and God?

DAY 3

O fire and deep well of charity!

RESPOND

What do you want to bring to God from your day?

RESOLVE

What resolution(s) do you wish to make for the coming day?

PRAY

Conclude by praying for God's grace in the coming day. You might do this by praying the Our Father, the Anima Christi, or the Suscipe prayer (see page 3).

DAY 4

PRAY

Lord, I want to give myself to you

Lord, I want to give myself to you,
body and soul, heart and mind and spirit
so that I may do what gladdens you.
In your mercy, grant me the grace
to have you continue in me
and through me your saving work.

St. Vincent de Paul

DATE

GIVE THANKS

What gifts have you received today? How have you been nourished, physically and spiritually?

EXAMINE

What did you do today? How did you treat yourself, others, and God?

DAY 4

Lord, I want to give myself to you

RESPOND

What do you want to bring to God from your day?

RESOLVE

What resolution(s) do you wish to make for the coming day?

PRAY

Conclude by praying for God's grace in the coming day. You might do this by praying the Our Father, the Anima Christi, or the Suscipe prayer (see page 3).

DAY 5

PRAY

Make my heart like yours!

Jesus, gentle and humble of heart,
make my heart like yours!

St. Thérèse of Lisieux

DATE

GIVE THANKS

What gifts have you received today? How have you been nourished, physically and spiritually?

EXAMINE

What did you do today? How did you treat yourself, others, and God?

DAY 5

Make my heart like yours!

RESPOND

What do you want to bring to God from your day?

RESOLVE

What resolution(s) do you wish to make for the coming day?

PRAY

Conclude by praying for God's grace in the coming day. You might do this by praying the Our Father, the Anima Christi, or the Suscipe prayer (see page 3).

DAY 6

PRAY

Christ be in my heart and mind

Christ be in my heart and mind,
Christ within my soul enshrined;
Christ control my wayward heart;
Christ abide and ne'er depart.

Christ my light and only way,
Christ my lantern night and day;
Christ be my unchanging friend,
Guide and shepherd to the end.

attributed to St. Patrick

DATE

GIVE THANKS

What gifts have you received today? How have you been nourished, physically and spiritually?

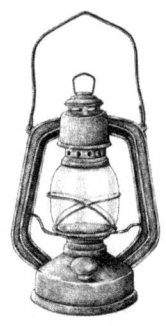

EXAMINE

What did you do today? How did you treat yourself, others, and God?

DAY 6

Christ be in my heart and mind

RESPOND

What do you want to bring to God from your day?

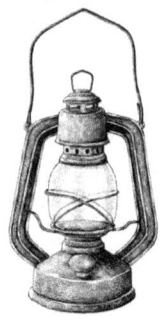

RESOLVE

What resolution(s) do you wish to make for the coming day?

PRAY

Conclude by praying for God's grace in the coming day. You might do this by praying the Our Father, the Anima Christi, or the Suscipe prayer (see page 3).

DAY 7

PRAY

For God alone my soul waits in silence

> For God alone my soul waits in silence,
>   for my hope is from him.
> He alone is my rock and my salvation,
>   my fortress; I shall not be shaken.
>
> *Psalm 62:5-6*

DATE

GIVE THANKS

What gifts have you received today? How have you been nourished, physically and spiritually?

EXAMINE

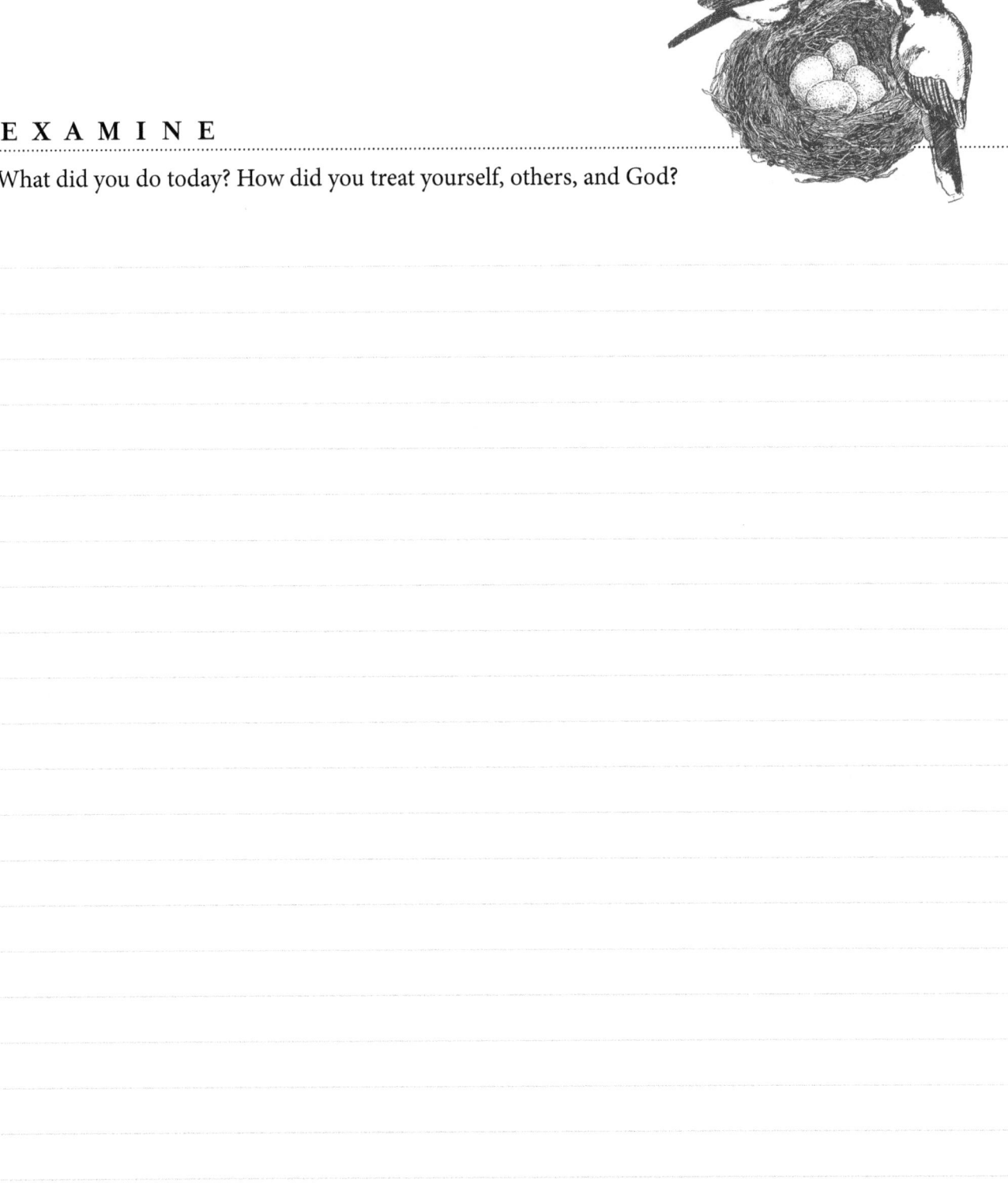

What did you do today? How did you treat yourself, others, and God?

DAY 7

For God alone my soul waits in silence

RESPOND

What do you want to bring to God from your day?

RESOLVE

What resolution(s) do you wish to make for the coming day?

PRAY

Conclude by praying for God's grace in the coming day. You might do this by praying the Our Father, the Anima Christi, or the Suscipe prayer (see page 3).

DAY 8

PRAY

Take from me everything

My Lord and my God,
take from me everything that distances me from you.
My Lord and my God,
give me everything that brings me close to you.
My Lord and my God,
detach me from myself to give my all to you.

St. Nicholas Flue

DATE

GIVE THANKS

What gifts have you received today? How have you been nourished, physically and spiritually?

EXAMINE

What did you do today? How did you treat yourself, others, and God?

DAY 8

Take from me everything

RESPOND

What do you want to bring to God from your day?

RESOLVE

What resolution(s) do you wish to make for the coming day?

PRAY

Conclude by praying for God's grace in the coming day. You might do this by praying the Our Father, the Anima Christi, or the Suscipe prayer (see page 3).

DAY 9

PRAY

Blessed be God

Blessed be God.
Blessed be his holy Name.
Blessed be Jesus Christ, true God and true Man.
Blessed be the name of Jesus.
Blessed be his most Sacred Heart.
Blessed be his most Precious Blood.
Blessed be Jesus in the most holy Sacrament of the altar.
Blessed be the Holy Spirit, the Paraclete.
Blessed be the great Mother of God, Mary most holy.
Blessed be her holy and Immaculate Conception.
Blessed be her glorious Assumption.
Blessed be the name of Mary, Virgin and Mother.
Blessed be St. Joseph, her most chaste spouse.
Blessed be God in his angels and in his saints. Amen.

The Divine Praises

DATE

GIVE THANKS

What gifts have you received today? How have you been nourished, physically and spiritually?

EXAMINE

What did you do today? How did you treat yourself, others, and God?

DAY 9

Blessed be God

RESPOND

What do you want to bring to God from your day?

RESOLVE

What resolution(s) do you wish to make for the coming day?

PRAY

Conclude by praying for God's grace in the coming day. You might do this by praying the Our Father, the Anima Christi, or the Suscipe prayer (see page 3).

DAY 10

PRAY

O Consuming Fire, Spirit of Love

O Consuming Fire, Spirit of Love,
overshadow me so that the Word may be,
as it were, incarnate again in my soul.
May I be for him a new humanity
in which he can renew all his mystery.

St. Elizabeth of the Trinity

DATE

GIVE THANKS

What gifts have you received today? How have you been nourished, physically and spiritually?

EXAMINE

What did you do today? How did you treat yourself, others, and God?

DAY 10

O Consuming Fire, Spirit of Love

RESPOND

What do you want to bring to God from your day?

RESOLVE

What resolution(s) do you wish to make for the coming day?

PRAY

Conclude by praying for God's grace in the coming day. You might do this by praying the Our Father, the Anima Christi, or the Suscipe prayer (see page 3).

DAY 11

PRAY

Only in you do I have everything

God, of your goodness,
give me yourself
for you are enough for me, and
I can ask for nothing less
that can pay you full worship.
And if I ask for anything less
always I am in want;
but only in you do I have everything.

Julian of Norwich

DATE

GIVE THANKS

What gifts have you received today? How have you been nourished, physically and spiritually?

EXAMINE

What did you do today? How did you treat yourself, others, and God?

DAY 11

Only in you do I have everything

RESPOND

What do you want to bring to God from your day?

RESOLVE

What resolution(s) do you wish to make for the coming day?

PRAY

Conclude by praying for God's grace in the coming day. You might do this by praying the Our Father, the Anima Christi, or the Suscipe prayer (see page 3).

DAY 12

PRAY

Wherever I go I shall find you

This I believe, O my God,
that wherever I go I shall find you,
and that there is no spot
not honored by your presence.

St. John Baptist de La Salle

DATE

GIVE THANKS

What gifts have you received today? How have you been nourished, physically and spiritually?

EXAMINE

What did you do today? How did you treat yourself, others, and God?

DAY 12

Wherever I go I shall find you

RESPOND

What do you want to bring to God from your day?

RESOLVE

What resolution(s) do you wish to make for the coming day?

PRAY

Conclude by praying for God's grace in the coming day. You might do this by praying the Our Father, the Anima Christi, or the Suscipe prayer (see page 3).

DAY 13

PRAY

Return, O my soul, to your rest

Gracious is the Lord, and righteous;
  our God is merciful.
The Lord protects the simple;
  when I was brought low, he saved me.
Return, O my soul, to your rest,
  for the Lord has dealt bountifully with you.

Psalm 116:5-7

DATE

GIVE THANKS

What gifts have you received today? How have you been nourished, physically and spiritually?

EXAMINE

What did you do today? How did you treat yourself, others, and God?

DAY 13

Return, O my soul, to your rest

RESPOND

What do you want to bring to God from your day?

RESOLVE

What resolution(s) do you wish to make for the coming day?

PRAY

Conclude by praying for God's grace in the coming day. You might do this by praying the Our Father, the Anima Christi, or the Suscipe prayer (see page 3).

DAY 14

PRAY

O give thanks to the Lord

This is the day that the Lord has made;
  let us rejoice and be glad in it.

You are my God, and I will give thanks to you;
  you are my God, I will extol you.

O give thanks to the Lord, for he is good,
  for his steadfast love endures forever.

Psalm 118:24, 29-20

DATE

GIVE THANKS

What gifts have you received today? How have you been nourished, physically and spiritually?

EXAMINE

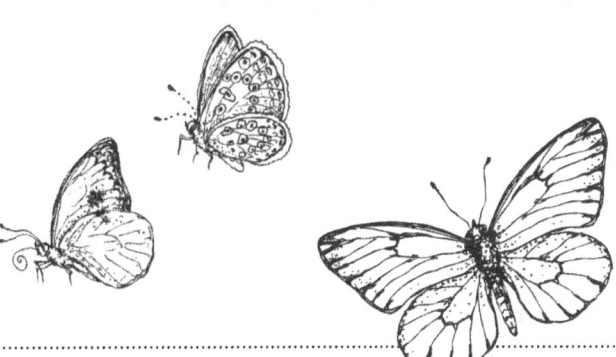

What did you do today? How did you treat yourself, others, and God?

DAY 14

O give thanks to the Lord

RESPOND

What do you want to bring to God from your day?

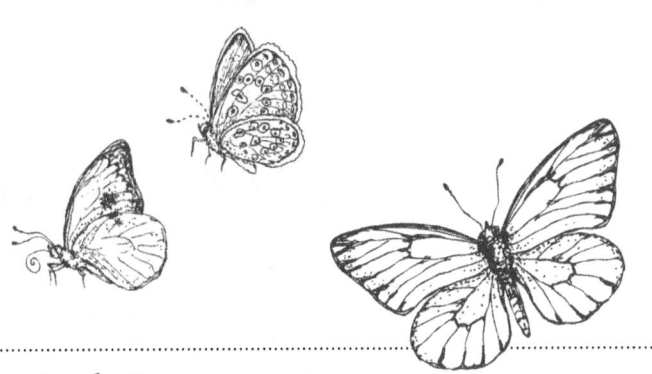

RESOLVE

What resolution(s) do you wish to make for the coming day?

PRAY

Conclude by praying for God's grace in the coming day. You might do this by praying the Our Father, the Anima Christi, or the Suscipe prayer (see page 3).

DAY 15

DATE

PRAY

You love me gratuitously

Eternal goodness,
you want me to gaze into you
and see that you love me,
to see that you love me gratuitously,
so that I may love everyone with the very same love....

God, come to our assistance! Amen.

St. Catherine of Siena

GIVE THANKS

What gifts have you received today? How have you been nourished, physically and spiritually?

EXAMINE

What did you do today? How did you treat yourself, others, and God?

DAY 15

You love me gratuitously

RESPOND

What do you want to bring to God from your day?

RESOLVE

What resolution(s) do you wish to make for the coming day?

PRAY

Conclude by praying for God's grace in the coming day. You might do this by praying the Our Father, the Anima Christi, or the Suscipe prayer (see page 3).

DAY 16

PRAY

Awaken and enlighten me, my Lord

Awaken and enlighten me, my Lord,
that I might know and love the blessings
which you ever propose to me,
and that I might understand
that you have moved to bestow favors on me
and have remembered me.

St. John of the Cross

DATE

GIVE THANKS

What gifts have you received today? How have you been nourished, physically and spiritually?

EXAMINE

What did you do today? How did you treat yourself, others, and God?

DAY 16

Awaken and enlighten me, my Lord

RESPOND

What do you want to bring to God from your day?

RESOLVE

What resolution(s) do you wish to make for the coming day?

PRAY

Conclude by praying for God's grace in the coming day. You might do this by praying the Our Father, the Anima Christi, or the Suscipe prayer (see page 3).

DAY 17

PRAY

My soul waits in silence

For God alone my soul waits in silence,
    for my hope is from him.
He alone is my rock and my salvation,
    my fortress; I shall not be shaken.
On God rests my deliverance and my honor;
    my mighty rock, my refuge is in God.

Trust in him at all times, O people;
    pour out your heart before him;
    God is a refuge for us.

Psalm 62:5-8

DATE

GIVE THANKS

What gifts have you received today? How have you been nourished, physically and spiritually?

EXAMINE

What did you do today? How did you treat yourself, others, and God?

DAY 17

My soul waits in silence

RESPOND

What do you want to bring to God from your day?

RESOLVE

What resolution(s) do you wish to make for the coming day?

PRAY

Conclude by praying for God's grace in the coming day. You might do this by praying the Our Father, the Anima Christi, or the Suscipe prayer (see page 3).

DAY 18

PRAY

Destroy me, O Lord

Destroy me, O Lord,
and upon my ruins
build a monument
to your glory.

— St. Laura Montoya Upegui

DATE

GIVE THANKS

What gifts have you received today? How have you been nourished, physically and spiritually?

EXAMINE

What did you do today? How did you treat yourself, others, and God?

DAY 18

Destroy me, O Lord

RESPOND

What do you want to bring to God from your day?

RESOLVE

What resolution(s) do you wish to make for the coming day?

PRAY

Conclude by praying for God's grace in the coming day. You might do this by praying the Our Father, the Anima Christi, or the Suscipe prayer (see page 3).

DAY 19

PRAY

Here I am, the servant of the Lord

Here am I, the servant of the Lord;
let it be with me according to your word.

    Mary (Luke 1:38)

DATE

GIVE THANKS

What gifts have you received today? How have you been nourished, physically and spiritually?

EXAMINE

What did you do today? How did you treat yourself, others, and God?

DAY 19

Here I am, the servant of the Lord

RESPOND

What do you want to bring to God from your day?

RESOLVE

What resolution(s) do you wish to make for the coming day?

PRAY

Conclude by praying for God's grace in the coming day. You might do this by praying the Our Father, the Anima Christi, or the Suscipe prayer (see page 3).

DAY 20

PRAY

The new song of your grace

I know not the song of your praises,
till you teach it, my God, to me;
till I hear the still voice of your Spirit,
who speaks forever of thee;
till I hear the celestial singing,
and learn the new song of your grace,
and then I shall tell forth the marvels
I learned in your secret place.

Blessed Richard Rolle

DATE

GIVE THANKS

What gifts have you received today? How have you been nourished, physically and spiritually?

EXAMINE

What did you do today? How did you treat yourself, others, and God?

DAY 20

The new song of your grace

RESPOND

What do you want to bring to God from your day?

RESOLVE

What resolution(s) do you wish to make for the coming day?

PRAY

Conclude by praying for God's grace in the coming day. You might do this by praying the Our Father, the Anima Christi, or the Suscipe prayer (see page 3).

DAY 21

PRAY

I bless the Lord who gives me counsel

I bless the Lord who gives me counsel;
  in the night also my heart instructs me.
I keep the Lord always before me;
  because he is at my right hand, I shall not be moved.

Therefore my heart is glad, and my soul rejoices;
  my body also rests secure.

Psakm 16:7-9

DATE

GIVE THANKS

What gifts have you received today? How have you been nourished, physically and spiritually?

EXAMINE

What did you do today? How did you treat yourself, others, and God?

DAY 21

I bless the Lord who gives me counsel

RESPOND

What do you want to bring to God from your day?

RESOLVE

What resolution(s) do you wish to make for the coming day?

PRAY

Conclude by praying for God's grace in the coming day. You might do this by praying the Our Father, the Anima Christi, or the Suscipe prayer (see page 3).

DAY 22

PRAY

Inflame our hearts with your love!

O love eternal, my soul needs and chooses you eternally!
Ah, come Holy Spirit, and inflame our hearts with your love!

St. Francis de Sales

DATE

GIVE THANKS

What gifts have you received today? How have you been nourished, physically and spiritually?

EXAMINE

What did you do today? How did you treat yourself, others, and God?

DAY 22

Inflame our hearts with your love!

RESPOND

What do you want to bring to God from your day?

RESOLVE

What resolution(s) do you wish to make for the coming day?

PRAY

Conclude by praying for God's grace in the coming day. You might do this by praying the Our Father, the Anima Christi, or the Suscipe prayer (see page 3).

DAY 23

PRAY

You are our haven and our hope

You are holy, Lord, the only God,
   and your deeds are wonderful.

  .   .   .   .   .

Lord God, living and true.
You are love. You are wisdom.
You are humility. You are endurance.
You are rest. You are peace.
You are joy and gladness.
You are justice and moderation.
You are all our riches,
   and you suffice for us.

You are beauty.
You are gentleness.
You are our protector.
You are our guardian and defender.
You are our courage.
You are our haven and our hope.
You are our faith, our great consolation.
You are our eternal life,
   Great and Wonderful Lord,
God Almighty, Merciful Saviour.

St. Francis

GIVE THANKS

What gifts have you received today? How have you been nourished, physically and spiritually?

DATE

EXAMINE

What did you do today? How did you treat yourself, others, and God?

DAY 23

You are our haven and our hope

RESPOND

What do you want to bring to God from your day?

RESOLVE

What resolution(s) do you wish to make for the coming day?

PRAY

Conclude by praying for God's grace in the coming day. You might do this by praying the Our Father, the Anima Christi, or the Suscipe prayer (see page 3).

DAY 24

PRAY

Your face, Lord, do I seek

Hear, O Lord, when I cry aloud,
  be gracious to me and answer me!
"Come," my heart says, "seek his face!"
  Your face, Lord, do I seek.
  Do not hide your face from me.

Psalm 27:7-9

DATE

GIVE THANKS

What gifts have you received today? How have you been nourished, physically and spiritually?

EXAMINE

What did you do today? How did you treat yourself, others, and God?

DAY 24

Your face, Lord, do I seek.

RESPOND

What do you want to bring to God from your day?

RESOLVE

What resolution(s) do you wish to make for the coming day?

PRAY

Conclude by praying for God's grace in the coming day. You might do this by praying the Our Father, the Anima Christi, or the Suscipe prayer (see page 3).

DAY 25

PRAY

To you, O Lord, I lift up my soul

Gladden the soul of your servant,
    for to you, O Lord, I lift up my soul.
For you, O Lord, are good and forgiving,
    abounding in steadfast love to all who call on you.
Give ear, O Lord, to my prayer;
    listen to my cry of supplication.

Psalm 86:4-6

DATE

GIVE THANKS

What gifts have you received today? How have you been nourished, physically and spiritually?

EXAMINE

What did you do today? How did you treat yourself, others, and God?

DAY 25

To you, O Lord, I lift up my soul

RESPOND

What do you want to bring to God from your day?

RESOLVE

What resolution(s) do you wish to make for the coming day?

PRAY

Conclude by praying for God's grace in the coming day. You might do this by praying the Our Father, the Anima Christi, or the Suscipe prayer (see page 3).

DAY 26

PRAY

You see my heart

Jesus Christ, Lord of all things!
You see my heart, you know my desires.
Possess all that I am—you alone.
I am your sheep;
make me worthy to overcome the devil.

   St. Agatha

DATE

GIVE THANKS

What gifts have you received today? How have you been nourished, physically and spiritually?

EXAMINE

What did you do today? How did you treat yourself, others, and God?

DAY 26

You see my heart

RESPOND

What do you want to bring to God from your day?

RESOLVE

What resolution(s) do you wish to make for the coming day?

PRAY

Conclude by praying for God's grace in the coming day. You might do this by praying the Our Father, the Anima Christi, or the Suscipe prayer (see page 3).

DAY 27

DATE

PRAY

My soul is like the weaned child

O Lord, my heart is not lifted up,
  my eyes are not raised too high;
I do not occupy myself with things
  too great and too marvelous for me.
But I have calmed and quieted my soul,
  like a weaned child with its mother;
  my soul is like the weaned child that is with me.

Psalm 131:1-2

GIVE THANKS

What gifts have you received today? How have you been nourished, physically and spiritually?

EXAMINE

What did you do today? How did you treat yourself, others, and God?

DAY 27

My soul is like the weaned child

RESPOND

What do you want to bring to God from your day?

RESOLVE

What resolution(s) do you wish to make for the coming day?

PRAY

Conclude by praying for God's grace in the coming day. You might do this by praying the Our Father, the Anima Christi, or the Suscipe prayer (see page 3).

DAY 28

PRAY

My soul desires to wait on you

And now, Desire of my soul,
my soul desires to wait on you a little space,
and to taste and see how gracious you are, O Lord.
I implore your tender mercy
to give me peace and silence from all things,
whether outward or inward.

William of St-Thierry

DATE

GIVE THANKS

What gifts have you received today? How have you been nourished, physically and spiritually?

EXAMINE

What did you do today? How did you treat yourself, others, and God?

DAY 28

My soul desires to wait on you

RESPOND

What do you want to bring to God from your day?

RESOLVE

What resolution(s) do you wish to make for the coming day?

PRAY

Conclude by praying for God's grace in the coming day. You might do this by praying the Our Father, the Anima Christi, or the Suscipe prayer (see page 3).

DAY 29

PRAY

Teach my heart to see you

O Lord my God,
teach my heart this day where and how
   to see you,
where and how to find you.
You have made me and remade me,
and you have bestowed on me
all the good things I possess,
and still I do not know you.
I have not yet done that
for which I was made.

Teach me to seek you,
for I cannot seek you
unless you teach me,
or find you
unless you show yourself to me.
Let me seek you in my desire,
let me desire you in my seeking.
Let me find you by loving you,
let me love you when I find you.

St. Anselm

DATE

GIVE THANKS

What gifts have you received today? How have you been nourished, physically and spiritually?

EXAMINE

What did you do today? How did you treat yourself, others, and God?

DAY 29

Teach my heart to see you

RESPOND

What do you want to bring to God from your day?

RESOLVE

What resolution(s) do you wish to make for the coming day?

PRAY

Conclude by praying for God's grace in the coming day. You might do this by praying the Our Father, the Anima Christi, or the Suscipe prayer (see page 3).

DAY 30

PRAY

Let me live to you who are life itself

Govern everything by your wisdom, O Lord,
so that my soul may always be serving you
in the way you will and not as I choose.
Let me die to myself so that I may serve you;
let me live to you who are life itself.

   St. Teresa of Avila

DATE

GIVE THANKS

What gifts have you received today? How have you been nourished, physically and spiritually?

EXAMINE

What did you do today? How did you treat yourself, others, and God?

DAY 30

Let me live to you who are life itself

RESPOND

What do you want to bring to God from your day?

RESOLVE

What resolution(s) do you wish to make for the coming day?

PRAY

Conclude by praying for God's grace in the coming day. You might do this by praying the Our Father, the Anima Christi, or the Suscipe prayer (see page 3).